# TOZZER

## SPECIAL EDITION

Pete

send love/hate mail to pete-rob@tozzer.com

# Tozzer 2: Special Edition

## Published by Ablaze Media
### www.tozzer.com

ISBN: 0-9543008-1-5
Printed in Spain

# TOZZER 2

## SPECIAL EDITION

WRITER
## ROB DUNLOP

ARTIST
## PETER LUMBY

COLORIST
## ERIC ERBES

ABLAZE
MEDIA

# WHO'S WHO?

## Tozzer

This kid's had it tough. As a baby, he was sent away to a godforsaken trailer park, and was brought up by the meanest couple who ever wore comfortable shoes. But Tozzer had a dream: to become an illusionist. So he packed his bags and made his way to Hollywood. Now he's enrolled at the world-famous Boarboils School of Drama.

## Butch and Jodie

The foster parents. They might only see Tozzer during the holidays, but that's still too much for them. Words can't describe the extent of their hatred for the boy, and every time he puts on a magic show, they hate him just a little bit more.

## Morphine

The enigmatic school principal. He has a penchant for long leather coats, strange colored pills, and really deep rabbit holes.

## Rod and Hornie

A one-armed klutz and a wannabe porn star. They're a couple of misfits, but they're also Tozzer's buddies, and the three of them make a hell of a team.

## Fucky

Tozzer's friend, confidant and pet. Okay, his vocabulary might be limited, but he sure knows how to swing a meat cleaver.

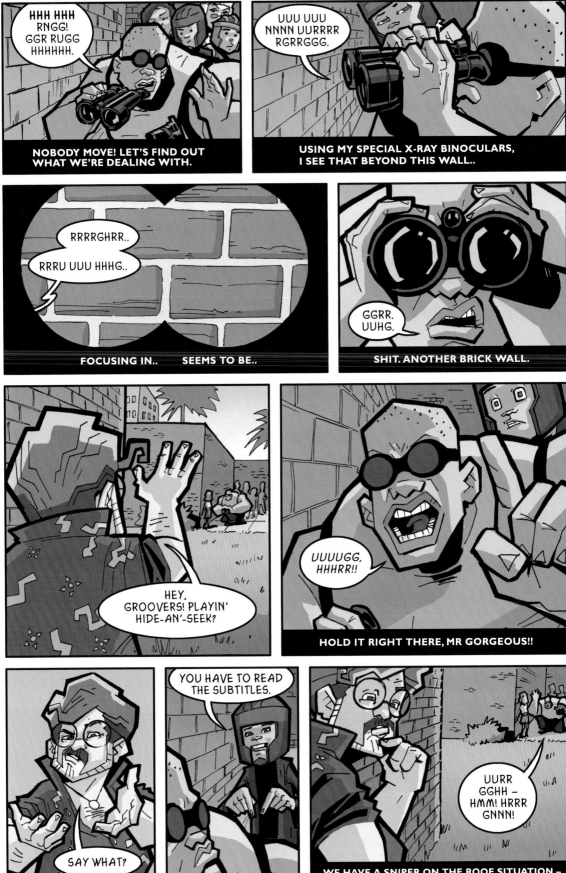

Here's an interview we did with Tim Cundle of *Mass Movement* magazine. It will give you a real insight into the working practices of the Tozzer team. Will it really? Will it fuck! But read it anyway. It's fun. You can read the full unedited version at www.mmzine.co.uk.

# AN INTERVIEW WITH MASS MOVEMENT

*Hitting the nail on the head - can you guys introduce yourselves?*

Rob: Hi, Tim. I'm Rob and I write the Tozzer scripts, which are passed on to Pete, who then does all the hard work. In fact I mostly just watch TV and learn how to redecorate and sell houses, which I'm sure will come in handy one day.

Pete: I'm Pete and I spend most of my time telling Rob he should get a girlfriend and lecturing him on his unhealthy fascination with Irish Boy bands. Just ask him a question about them, any question, he'll know the answer right off. As for me, well I'm affectionately known as the art gimp. I faithfully reproduce what's in Rob's odd shaped head.

Rob: As you can see, we have a great working relationship, and an enormous amount of respect for each other. There is absolutely no malice between me and that lard-ass pig-fucker.

*Which comes first - words or pictures, and how do you guys go about piecing each issue together? Any dissent in the ranks - and if so, how do you settle the disputes? Pistols at dawn?*

Rob: Words come first. I give Pete a full script, and he tells me where it sucks and where it doesn't suck quite so much, and I try to remove the excess suckiness with a blowtorch and pliers. When the script's as suck-free as possible, Pete takes over and gets drawing. He also does the inking, and the lettering. Like I said, I mostly just watch TV.

Pete: Harmonious, if you call arguing the color of the sky harmonious. We disagree on just about every aspect of the creative process, then after spending an inordinate amount of time debating politely who's the bigger c\*\*t, him or me, we usually find that actually we both had the same point of view all along. I don't know how, but it seems to work.

*What do you think it is about fame that drives people to want it above all other things?*

Rob: I blame Bob Monkhouse. *Opportunity Knocks* was the obvious precursor to *Pop Idol* and *The X-Factor*. It might have had more charm and better production values, but Bob's show paved the way for the horrors that are shown on TV today. TV - now that has a lot to answer for. Let's take *Friends*. You can bum around, chill with your homies and be an out of work actor or failed musician and still afford to live in a huge flat in one of the most expensive cities in the world. Or there's the *Simpsons*. You can be the most stupid, lazy, useless person on the planet, live off beer and donuts, yet still have your own car, detached house in a leafy suburb, and a gorgeous trophy wife with stunning blue hair. What I'm trying to say here is millions of people are told every day by their TVs that they can have everything they want and hard work or talent are not requirements. I am one of these people. I want it all, now, and I ain't lifting my fat fucking fingers to get it!

Pete: Does that answer the question?

Rob: No, probably not.

*Which comic book hero is the ultimate creation?*

Rob: I dunno, could you give me a clue?

Pete: I'd say there is only one clear-cut ultimate hero and that's Screw-on Head, from *The Amazing Screw-on Head*, by Mike Mignola. I know it may go against the grain, but let's face it he's just more entertaining than any member of *Watchmen*. Come on, Mike let's see more Screw-on! And where's the

*How do you think the comics industry and comics in general have evolved over the last decade?*

Rob: I think it's best to look at the last four or five years, mostly because that's all I know about. There have been a couple of obvious influences on the business in recent years. One has been the growing strength of graphic novels, both in comic shops and regular bookshops.

Rob: The other influence is all the comic-film adaptations, from *Ghost World* to *Spiderman* to *Hellboy*. Writers and artists have seen Hollywood's new love affair with comics and we've got something of a gold-rush on our hands. Some great talent has come to the medium as a means of breaking into the film industry, so you've got an increasing number of independent titles with slick production values which are basically movie proposals. This is all good for us, as we're part of an industry which is slowly finding its feet again.

*Pro-Wrestling. Serious sports entertainment or just a glorified soap opera?*

Rob: Serious sports entertainment. Anyone who dresses like a third rate comic book villain and takes enough steroids to kill a horse has got to be taken seriously. Their attire reflects their sanity and their drug intake reflects their ability to inflict pain on skinny wimps like myself.

Pete: Rob's right you know... he is a skinny wimp.

*Conspiracy theories. Are you believers?*

Rob: Normally, I don't believe in conspiracies. Princess Diana being abducted by Danish vampire-lizards so they could turn her into jelly and sell her as Fry's Turkish Delight - that, however, has a ring of truth about it. I had a bit of Turkish Delight the other day, and I swear I got a mild cocaine high from it. You'll notice that "Princess Diana" is itself an anagram of "tasty confectionery", give or take a few letters. Make of that what you will.

Pete: How do you know what a mild cocaine high would feel like, Rob?

Rob: Coz you told me! You said it was like having 10 cups of Irish coffee while Angelina Jolie's sat on your shoulders saying "You're cooler than Sean Connery and your conversation makes my pussy wet".

Pete: I never said that! Anyway, moving on... you got any more of that Turkish Delight?

*What's next for you guys and "Tozzer"*

Rob: We've got 2 projects coming up which are nothing to do with Tozzer, and they are very different from what we've done before. By the time Pete's finished the artwork on Tozzer 2, I'll have completed the graphic novel I'm writing now, and I've written another graphic novel which needs a little tweaking. So Pete will work on one, and we'll get other artists on board for the other.

Pete: After that, the plan is for me to get stuck into Tozzer 3, which should be released in 2006 sometime. Tozzer 3 might be called something else though, as we're thinking of turning it into a series of self-contained stories as opposed to one story chopped up into pieces. But we'll see how things pan out. We'll probably stick to the graphic novel format for everything that isn't Tozzer.

*Anything that you'd like to add...*

Rob: Ketchup, if you have any.

Pete: Check out Tozzer.com and buy our comics, or

# Pencils

Ok, here's how a typical page of Tozzer is done. After reading Rob's script, I'll start working on thumbnail layouts. These are usually small and illegible - it helps the creative process.

Then I work up the final page in rough blue pencil. There's a very clever reason for this, which I'll reveal later. By the way, my favorite color is turquoise.

Now I'm onto the exciting bit: tracing. I use three basic types of pen to ink over the pencil sketch - a thin one, a fat one and a seriously obese one for large areas of black. I listen to the uplifting melodies of Dido, to get me in the mood.

When the inking's done, I scan the page into my super-computer and - here's the clever bit - I remove the blue pencil lines in Photoshop. And that's it finished! Um, except for laying out the text, sound effects and making speech bubbles... Man, how long does it take to make a comic?! It's not even colored yet! I'm going back to breeding budgerigars.

Pete

Here's some early sketches of Tozzer and Hornie. I did loads more development sketches but most of them are frankly too crap to print.

**TOZZER**

**HORNIE**

enlarge Head.

reduce hands.

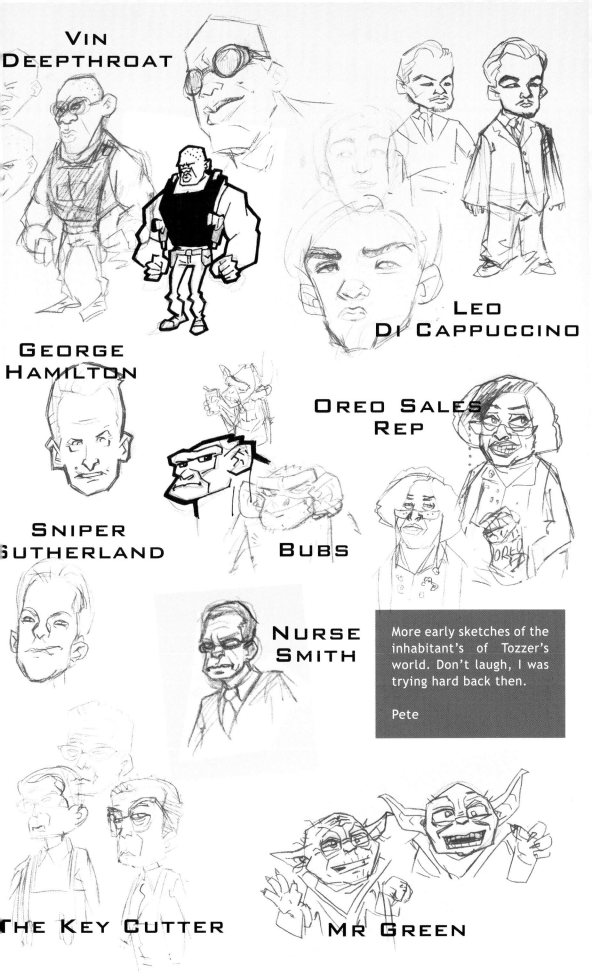

VIN
DEEPTHROAT

LEO
DI CAPPUCCINO

GEORGE
HAMILTON

OREO SALES
REP

SNIPER
SUTHERLAND

BUBS

NURSE
SMITH

More early sketches of the inhabitant's of Tozzer's world. Don't laugh, I was trying hard back then.

Pete

THE KEY CUTTER

MR GREEN

# COVERS

Episode II: Ate Mile

Episode III: Phone Boobs

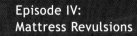
Episode IV:
Mattress Revulsions

Episode V: Hulk Fiction

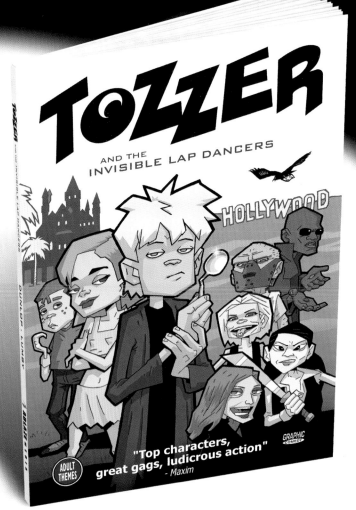